PILLOW PIZZAZZ™

Edited by Carolyn S. Vagts

Annie's™

Introduction

Pillows are the perfect complement to any room. If you're looking for a weekend project to freshen up a tired sofa or boring duvet, *Pillow Pizzazz* may be the answer. Give a room a new look with a few quilted pillows and do it on a budget. Most pillows can be made in a short amount of time—well, depending on your skill level—and many times with your stashed fabrics. Pillows offer many options and opportunities for designing, skill building and gift giving, and they can be a quilter's inspiration.

This book presents you with a wide variety of styles, shapes and sizes. It has something for everyone. There are traditional pieced, scrappy, modern, and bright and fun. Making a pillow is an excellent way to try a new technique, and the commitment of your time is less than making a full-fledged quilt. Thumb through these pages and see all the possibilities awaiting you. *Pillow Pizzazz* is a collection of 12 sets of gorgeous pillows. Also check out the how-to ideas for whole-cloth quilting with a twist. And as an added bonus, you can turn your practice pieces into one-of-a-kind pillows.

You select the fabrics and our designers supply you with the inspiration and the instructions. What could be nicer?

Happy quilting!

Carolyn S. Vagts

Table of Contents

Instant Classic, page 22

Scrappy String Pllows, page 10

Abacus Pillow

Design by Holly Daniels

Monochromatic can be fun and stylish when you choose to make this pillow.

Project Specifications
Skill Level: Beginner
Pillow Size: 14" x 14"

Materials
Note: Materials and instructions listed are for one pillow

- ⅛ yard each coordinating green and dark green solids
- ¼ yard each coordinating light and medium green prints
- ⅝ yard coordinating fabric for back
- ⅝ yard muslin
- ⅝ yard thin batting
- 14"-square pillow form
- Thread
- Iron-on adhesive (optional)
- Fabric basting spray (optional)
- Basic sewing tools and supplies

Cutting
1. Prepare template from circle pattern provided and cut eight F circles from green solid for appliqué referring to Fusible Appliqué on page 4.

2. Cut two 1" x fabric width dark green solid strips; subcut strips into three 1" x 16" E strips.

3. Cut one 4¾" by fabric width strip from light green print; subcut one 4¾" x 16" A strip.

4. Trim remainder of light green print strip to 3½" wide and cut one 3½" x 16" C strip.

5. Cut one 4¾" by fabric width strip from medium green print; subcut one 4¾" x 16" B strip.

6. Trim remainder of medium green print strip to 3½" wide and cut one 3½" x 16" D strip.

7. Cut one 14½" square for pillow back from coordinating fabric.

8. Cut one each 16"-square of muslin and batting. make 12 rows.

Pillow-Top Assembly
1. Sew strips A–D alternately with E right sides together along long edges referring to Figure 1. Press seams away from E strips.

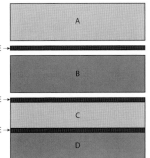
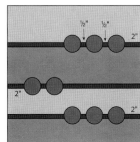

Figure 1   **Figure 2**

2. Position three circles centered on each top and bottom E strip, ½" apart and 2" from the pillow-top right side as shown in Figure 2. Appliqué circles in place referring to Fusible Appliqué on page 4.

3. Position two circles centered on the middle E strip, ½" apart and 2" from the pillow-top left side, again referring to Figure 2. Appliqué circles in place.

4. Layer batting square between muslin square and wrong side of pillow top. Baste layers together with thread, safety pins or fabric basting spray. Quilt as desired.

5. Evenly trim quilted pillow top to 14½" square as shown in Figure 3. **Note:** *Circles will be 1¼" from pillow raw edges after trimming.*

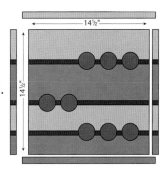

Figure 3

3

6. Position pillow top right sides together with pillow back matching edges and stitch all four sides leaving an 8" opening in one side for turning.

7. Trim corners and turn right side out, gently pushing corners out. Press edges, pressing opening seam allowance to inside.

8. Insert 14"-square pillow form into pillow through opening. Ladder-stitch opening closed by hand as shown in Figure 4 to complete pillow. ■

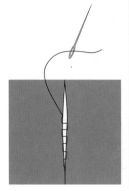

Figure 4

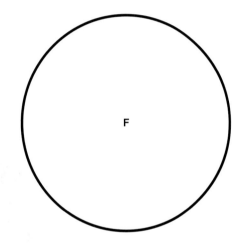

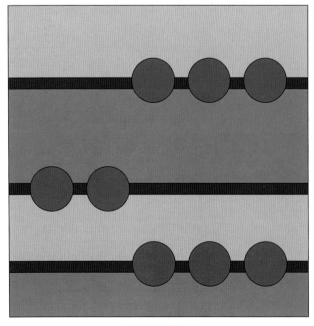

Abacus Pillow
Placement Diagram 14" x 14"

Fusible Appliqué

One of the easiest ways to appliqué is the fusible web method. Paper-backed fusible web motifs are fused to the wrong side of fabric, cut out and then fused to a foundation fabric and stitched by hand or machine. You can use this method for raw- or turned-edge appliqué.

Raw-Edge Fusible Appliqué

Note: If the appliqué motif is directional, it should be reversed for fusible appliqué. If doing several identical appliqué motifs, trace reversed motif shapes onto template material to make reusable templates.

1. Use templates or trace the appliqué motif shapes onto paper side of paper-backed fusible web. Leave at least ½" between shapes. Cut out shapes, leaving a margin around traced lines.

2. Follow manufacturer's instructions and fuse shapes to wrong side of fabric as indicated on pattern for color and number to cut.

3. Cut out appliqué shapes on traced lines and remove paper backing from fusible web.

4. Again following manufacturer's instructions, arrange and fuse pieces to foundation referring to appliqué motif included in pattern.

5. Hand- or machine-stitch around edges. Some stitch possibilities are satin or zigzag, buttonhole, blanket or running stitch.

Turned-Edge Fusible Appliqué

1. Prepare paper-backed fusible web shapes as in step 1 of Raw-Edge Fusible Appliqué except cut out shapes along the traced lines.

2. Apply fusible web shapes to wrong side of fabric as for raw-edge fusible appliqué, spacing shapes at least ½" apart.

3. Cut out appliqué shapes approximately ¼" away from fusible web edge. Before removing paper backing, press ¼" fabric margin toward fusible web. Remove paper backing.

4. Apply appliqué shapes to foundation as for raw-edge fusible appliqué.

5. Hand- or machine-stitch folded edges down. Some possibilities are buttonhole, blanket or blind hemstitches. Choose matching thread and a stitch that can be hidden if you do not want to see the stitches. ■

Jelly Roll Bolster Pillow

Design by Jen Eskridge

Make this bolster with 2½" precut strips, adding a little punch to any room.

Project Specifications

Skill Level: Beginner
Bolster Size: 8" x 24"

Materials

Note: Materials and instructions listed are for one pillow.

- 14 precut 2½" coordinating strips
- ½ yard ½" cotton cord
- 8" x 24" bolster pillow insert
- ½ yard 1"-wide hook-and-loop tape
- Thread
- Freezer paper
- Zipper foot
- Basic sewing tools and supplies

Cutting

1. Cut eight 2" by fabric with A strips light blue tonal.

2. Cut seven 2" by fabric width B strips light green tonal.

3. Cut four 5" by fabric width strips pink print; subcut strips into (32) 5" C squares.

4. Cut seven 2" by fabric width strips dark pink tonal; subcut strips into (128) 2" D squares.

5. Cut five 1½" by fabric width I/J strips dark pink tonal.

Preparation & Cutting

1. Use circle template to draw two 8¾"-diameter circles on dull side of freezer paper and cut out on lines. Set aside.

2. Join 12 (2½") coordinating strips right sides together along long edges. Press seams in one direction. *Note: Finishing the raw edges of the strips with an over-edge stitch or a serger will eliminate fraying on the inside of your pillow cover.*

3. Referring to Figure 1, mark and cut one 24½" x 29" rectangle from pieced strips for bolster body.

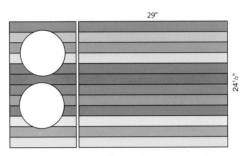

Figure 1

4. Press freezer paper circle templates shiny side down on right side of pieced-strip remnant, again referring to Figure 1. Cut around circles to make bolster ends.

5. Trim two remaining 2½" strips to 1½" x 28" strips.

Completing the Bolster

1. Stitch a 1⅜" double-turned hem along the 24½" ends of the body rectangle by pressing ¼" to wrong side and then pressing 1⅛" to wrong side; edges-stitch on first fold as shown in Figure 2.

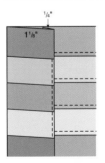

Figure 2

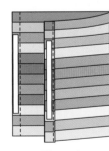

Figure 3

2. Trim hook-and-loop tape to 15" long. Center hook side on right side of one hemmed end of bolster body as shown in Figure 3 and stitch around perimeter.

3. Center loop side on wrong side of opposite hemmed end and stitch around perimeter, again referring to Figure 3.

8

4. Join hook-and-loop pieces as they will be joined in the finished pillow cover. Pin the loose ends past the hook-and-loop tape closed.

5. Referring to Figure 4, stitch across hems beyond hook-and-loop tape and along hem edge as shown in red to reinforce bolster closure.

Figure 4

6. Fold bolster body in fourths along the 29" side and edge-clip at each fold.

7. Prepare the bolster end cord referring to Finishing Pillow Edges With Covered Cord and using the 1½" x 28" coordinating strips.

8. Fold each 8¾" circle into fourths and edge-clip at each fold.

9. Baste the cord to the right side of each circle, stitching close to the covered cord stitching line and referring to Finishing Pillow Edges With Covered Cord or Trim, on page 9, to meet cord ends at one of the clips as shown in Figure 5.

Figure 5

10. Turn bolster body wrong side out and generously pin circles right sides together to the bolster body tube, matching the clips as shown in Figure 6. *Note: Positioning the cord beginning/end seam at the body closure, places both of these elements at the back of the bolster when displayed.*

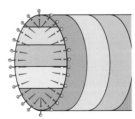

Figure 6

11. Position zipper foot close to cord and sew end circles to bolster body. Finish seams with zigzag, over-edge stitch or serger.

12. Turn right side out and insert 8" x 24" bolster pillow insert. ■

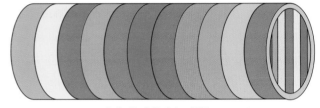

Jelly Roll Bolster Pillow
Placement Diagram 8" x 24"

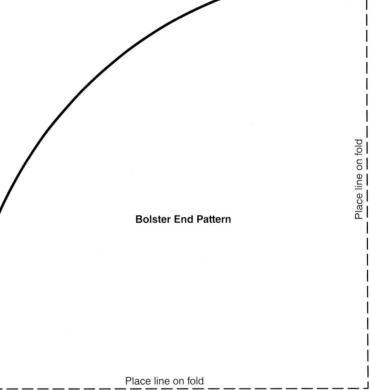

Place line on fold

Bolster End Pattern

Place line on fold

Finishing Pillow Edges With Covered Cord or Trim

A few simple steps added to the final construction of a pillow can change the look of any pillow. Inserting fabric-covered cord around the edges of a pillow gives a tailored look for a more formal setting, and adding home decor trims may provide elegance or whimsy.

1. Cut bias or straight-grain fabric strips approximately three times the circumference of the cord width and at least 4" longer than the length needed or as indicated in the pattern. For example, if using ½" cord on the outside edges of a 14" square pillow you will need a strip 1½" wide and 60" long.

2. Beginning approximately 2" from the strip end, fold the strip around the cord wrong sides together matching the strip edges. Pin close to the cord for a few inches to hold when beginning to stitch.

3. Keeping the cord inside the folded strip and strip edges matching for entire length, use a zipper foot (or cording foot) to slowly stitch close to the cord as shown in Figure 1. When complete, the fabric strip should extend beyond the ends of the cord.

Figure 1

4. If necessary, trim the covered-cord seam allowance to the same seam allowance being used to stitch the pillow edges together as shown in Figure 2.

← ¼"

Figure 2

5. Position and pin one end of the covered cord at the center of one side of the pillow. Pull the empty fabric strip ends toward the pillow edges as shown in Figure 3. Continue pinning the covered cord to the pillow-top edges.

Figure 3

6. To reduce bulk where the cord ends meet, pin one covered cord end to meet the other end, again pulling the empty fabric strip ends toward the pillow edges, again referring to Figure 3. *Note: You could also overlap the strip and have the cord meet in the interior of the folded strip as shown in Figure 4.*

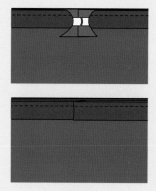

Figure 4

7. Baste the covered cord to the pillow top, matching raw edges.

8. Layer the pillow top and back as instructed in pattern and pin edges close to cord. Stitch as close as possible to cording.

You can add home decor trims to pillow edges in the same manner if they include a seam allowance. ■

Scrappy String Pillows

Designs by Julie Weaver

The chic look of neutral fabrics and sashing make these elegant string pillows a boost to any decor.

Project Specifications

Skill Level: Confident Beginner
Brown Pillow Size: 24" x 16" with flange
Black Pillow Size: 22" x 22" with flange

Brown Pillow

Materials

- Assorted scraps or fat quarters cream, white and tan
- ⅝ yard white solid
- ⅞ yard dark brown tonal
- ⅔ yard muslin
- Lightweight batting 28" x 20"
- 12" x 20" pillow insert
- Thread
- Fabric basting spray (optional)
- Basic sewing tools and supplies

Cutting

1. Cut an assortment of strips varying in width from ¾"–1½" by 10" long from cream, white and tan scraps or fat quarters.

2. Cut one 7" by fabric width white solid strip; subcut strip into one 6" x 7" A rectangle, one 7" x 10" B rectangle and one 7" x 9" D rectangle.

3. Cut one 10" by fabric width white solid strip; subcut strip into one 10" C square and one 5" x 16" E rectangle.

4. Cut two 1½" by fabric width dark brown tonal strips; subcut one strip each into 1½" x 14½" F, 1½" x 12½" G, 1½" x 8½" H and 1½" x 5½" I strips for sashing.

5. Cut three 2½" by fabric width dark brown tonal strips; subcut strips into two each 2½" x 28" J and 2½" x 20" K strips for pillow flanges.

6. Cut one 14½" by fabric width dark brown tonal strip; subcut strip into two 14½" x 16½" L rectangles for pillow backs.

7. Cut one 20" x 28" rectangle muslin for backing.

Completing Pillow Top

1. Refer to Foundation Piecing, on page 15, to make five pieced units using white solid A–E pieces for foundations and assortment of cream, white and tan strips. Trim completed pieced units to the following sizes: 4½" x 5½" A, 5½" x 8½" B, 8½" square C, 5½" x 7½" D and 3½" x 14½" E.

2. Stitch sashing strips F–I and pieced units A–E together as shown in Figure 1 to make the pieced center.

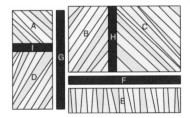

Figure 1

3. Center and sew K borders to short sides of pieced center, beginning and ending stitching ¼" from the center corner and backstitching as shown in Figure 2. *Note: K borders will extend past edges of pieced center.* Repeat with J borders on the long sides of pieced center. Press seams toward borders.

Figure 2

4. Fold and pin pillow top right sides together at a 45-degree angle on one corner, matching seam lines and border edges as shown in Figure 3. Place a straightedge along the fold and lightly mark a line across the J and K ends.

Figure 3

5. Stitch along the line, backstitching to secure. Trim seam to ¼" and press open to miter a border corner as shown in Figure 4.

Figure 4

6. Repeat steps 4 and 5 to miter all four border corners.

7. Layer batting between completed pillow top and muslin backing rectangle. Spray-baste, thread-baste or pin layers together. Quilt as desired. *Note: Do not quilt in-the-ditch around the pillow center at this time.*

8. Trim batting and backing to the same size as pillow top.

Completing the Pillow

1. Press ¼" to wrong side of L along one 16½" edge. Press 1¼" to wrong side of same edge to make hem as shown in Figure 5.

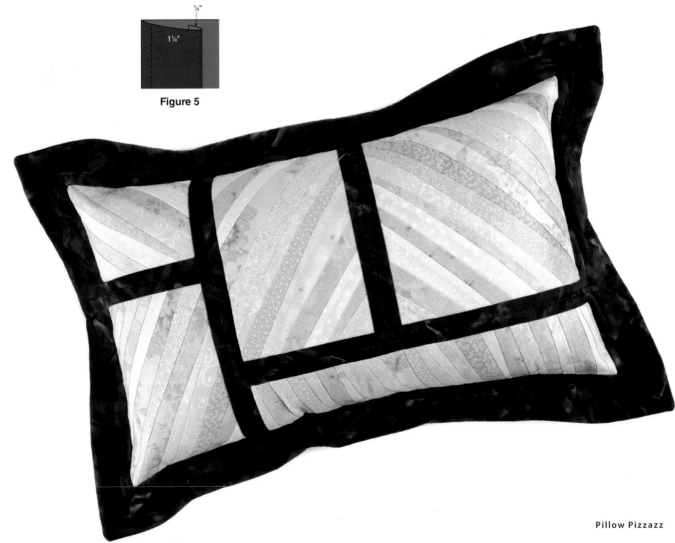

Figure 5

2. Stitch ¼" from second pressed edge and edges-titch first pressed edge, again referring to Figure 5. Repeat steps 1 and 2 with second L pillow back.

3. Position and pin L pillow backs right sides together with completed pillow top matching raw edges and overlapping hemmed edges.

4. Stitch around all raw edges; trim seams and corners. Turn pillow right side out and press.

5. Stitch in-the-ditch around the pillow pieced center creating a pillow flange as shown in Figure 6. Stitch again ¼" from the previous stitching line on the flange, again referring to Figure 6.

Figure 6

6. Insert pillow form to complete pillow.

Black Pillow

Materials
- Assorted scraps or fat quarters black and gray
- ⅝ yard gray solid
- 1⅛ yards black stripe
- ¾ yard muslin
- Lightweight batting 26" x 26"
- 18"-square pillow form
- Thread
- Fabric basting spray (optional)
- Basic sewing tools and supplies

Cutting
1. Cut an assortment of strips varying in width from ¾"–1½" by 10" long from black and gray scraps or fat quarters.

2. Cut one 7" by fabric width gray solid strip; subcut strip into two 7" x 8" A and C rectangles and one each 7" x 9" D and 5" x 7" F rectangle.

3. Cut one 8" by fabric width gray solid strip; subcut strip into one each 8" B square, 8" x 14" G rectangle and 6" x 14" E rectangle.

4. Cut two 1½" by fabric width black stripe strips; subcut strips into two each 1½" x 12½" J and 1½" x 5½" H sashing strips and one each 1½" x 6½" I and 1½" x 18½" K sashing strips

5. Cut four 2½ by fabric width black stripe strips. Subcut strips into four 2½" x 25" L border strips.

6. Cut one 22½" by fabric width black stripe strip; subcut strip into two 13½" x 22½" M rectangles for pillow backs.

7. Cut one 22" square muslin for backing.

Completing the Pillow Top
1. Refer to Foundation Piecing to make seven pieced units using gray solid A–G pieces for foundations and assortment of black and gray strips. Trim completed pieced units to the following sizes: A (5½" x 6½"), B (6½" square), C (5½" x 6½"), D (5½" x 7½"), E (4½" x 12½"), F (3½" x 5½") and G (6½" x 12½").

2. Stitch sashing strips H–K and pieced units A–G together as shown in Figure 7 to make the pieced center.

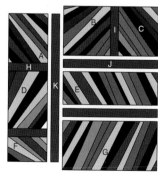

Figure 7

3. Referring to steps 3–6 in Completing the Pillow Top for the brown pillow, add the L border strips to the black pillow pieced center stitching mitered corners.

4. Layer batting between completed pillow top and muslin backing rectangle. Spray-baste, thread-baste or pin layers together. Quilt as desired. ***Note:*** *Do not quilt in-the-ditch around the pillow center at this time.*

5. Trim batting and backing to the same size as pillow top.

Completing the Pillow

1. Referring to steps 1–6 of Completing the Pillow for the brown pillow, use M pieces for the pillow back and black pillow quilted top to complete a black pillow. ■

Scrappy String Pillow
Placement Diagram 24" x 16"

Scrappy String Pillow
Placement Diagram 22" x 22"

Foundation Piecing

Any time you stitch small fabric shapes to a piece of fabric or paper to create a pieced design you are foundation piecing. You can use these simple instructions for string piecing (stitching uneven widths of fabric strips to a piece of base fabric or foundation) or for crazy quilting (odd fabric shapes sewn onto a fabric foundation).

1. Cut a piece of foundation fabric the size indicated in the pattern instructions from muslin or other compatible solid-color fabric.

2. Select a precut strip and pin it along a diagonal of the foundation square as shown in Figure 1. Trim strip to a manageable length, if necessary, with extra extending at each end, again referring to Figure 1.

Figure 1

3. Select another strip and pin right sides together with first strip, trimming excess as in step 2. Stitch ¼" from the edge of the pinned strips as shown in Figure 2.

Figure 2

4. Press the top strip to the right side as shown in Figure 3.

Figure 3

5. Continue adding strips to the foundation piece in this manner until the foundation is completely covered as shown in Figure 4. *Note: For crazy quilting, use odd shapes beginning at the center of the foundation piece and adding pieces in a circular manner.*

Figure 4

6. Trim the stitched foundation piece to the size indicated in the pattern, as shown in Figure 5, to complete the block unit. ■

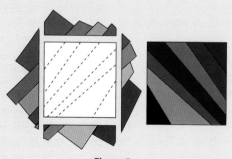

Figure 5

Annie's, Berne, Indiana 46711 Clotilde.com

Prairie Paths

Design by Carol Streif

Traditional prairie points take on a very upbeat look when used in paths to accent the simple seams of this design.

Project Specifications
Skill Level: Beginner
Pillow Size: 16" x 16"

Materials
Note: Materials and instructions listed are for one pillow.

- ¼ yard each 7 coordinating plaids
- ⅝ yard batik print
- 16"-square pillow form
- Neutral-color all-purpose thread
- Basic sewing tools and supplies

Cutting
1. Cut one 16½" by fabric width batik print strip; subcut strip into one 6½" x 16½" A rectangle, four 3" x 16½" B rectangles and two 11" x 16½" D rectangles.

2. Cut one 4" by fabric width strip from each coordinating plaid; subcut each strip into four 4" C squares.

Completing the Pillow
1. Fold and press C squares in half wrong sides together forming a rectangle as shown in Figure 1. Fold upper left corner to bottom center, again referring to Figure 1; press. Repeat with upper right corner, again referring to Figure 1, to make a prairie point; press.

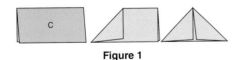

Figure 1

2. Repeat to make a total of 28 prairie points.

3. Select one of each color prairie point and arrange evenly as desired on one long edge of B rectangle starting at center as shown in Figure 2. Baste along seam line. Repeat to make second prairie point strip.

4. Repeat arrangement on opposite edge of two remaining B rectangles to make a reversed prairie point strip, again referring to Figure 2. Baste along seam line.

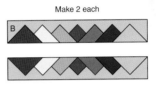

Make 2 each

Figure 2

5. Stitch matching prairie point strips to one 16½" side of the A rectangle referring to Figure 3. Stitch reversed prairie point strips to opposite side of A, again referring to Figure 3, to complete the pillow top.

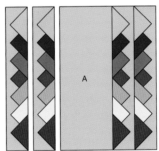

Figure 3

6. Fold and press ¼" and then 1" to wrong side of 16½" side of D as shown in Figure 4. Edgestitch along first fold to hem. Repeat with second D rectangle.

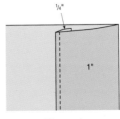

Figure 4

7. Stitch a D rectangle to opposite prairie point sides of pillow top matching raw 16½" edges as shown in Figure 5. Finish all raw edges with zigzag or overedge stitch. Press seams toward pillow top.

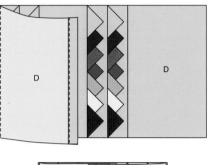

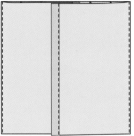

Figure 5

8. Fold and pin D rectangles over pillow top right sides together, overlapping and matching raw edges, again referring to Figure 5.

9. Stitch top and bottom of pillow, trim corners and finish raw edges. Turn right side out through opening and insert the 16"-square pillow form. ■

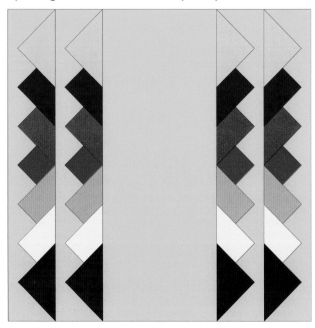

Prairie Paths
Placement Diagram 16" x 16"

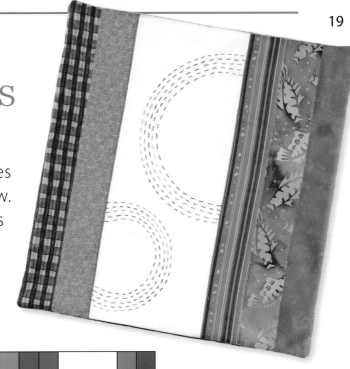

Bright Stitches

Design by Missy Shepler

Precut strips and simple embroidery stitches on a plain white insert create a lovely pillow. Just imagine how many color combinations you could use!

Project Specifications
Skill Level: Beginner
Pillow Size: 16" x 16"

Materials
- 8 precut 2½" coordinating strips
- ⅞ yard solid white
- ¾ yard 45"-wide lightweight batting
- 16"-square pillow form
- 3 (⅝") buttons
- Coordinating colors size 8 pearl cotton
- Thread
- Tapestry needle
- Water soluble fabric marker
- Walking foot (optional)
- Buttonhole foot (optional)
- Basic sewing tools and supplies

Cutting
1. Cut (15) 2½" x 18" A strips from coordinating 2½" by fabric width precut strips.

2. Cut one 18" by fabric width strip white solid; subcut strip into one each 18" C square, 9" x 18" D rectangle and 11½" x 18" E rectangle.

3. Cut one 6½" by fabric width strip white solid; subcut strip into one 6½" x 18" B rectangle.

4. From batting, cut one 18" square pillow front and two 11" x 18" pillow back rectangles.

Completing the Pillow Front
1. Stitch two A strips to one 18" side of B and three A strips to the opposite side of B to make pillow front as shown in Figure 1. Press seams toward A strips.

2. Layer 18" square of batting between C square right side down, and pillow front, right side up; baste together. Use a walking foot to quilt close to seams as shown in Figure 2.

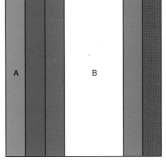

Figure 1

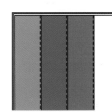

Figure 2

3. Trim the pillow front down to 16½" square and staystitch ⅛" from edges.

4. Draw two or three partial circles on the center white panel of the pillow front with a water-soluble fabric marker referring to the Placement Diagram and photos. Draw 3–5 concentric circles ¼" apart within the first circle. *Note: Use a round object as a template, like a plate or lid to draw the circles.*

5. Use a running stitch and a single 30" strand of pearl cotton to hand-quilt the concentric circles as shown in Figure 3. Bury thread ends between the quilt layers to secure.

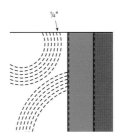

¼"

Figure 3

Annie's, Berne, Indiana 46711 Clotilde.com

Completing the Pillow Back

1. Stitch five A strips right sides together lengthwise to 18" right side of D to make A-D unit as shown in Figure 4. Press seam allowances toward A.

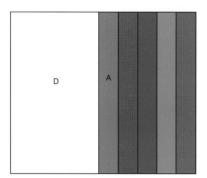

Figure 4

2. Fold and press the A-D unit in half wrong sides together to make the upper pillow back as shown in Figure 5. Align seams and stitch just below the seam line to form the button flap, again referring to Figure 5.

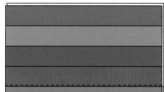

Figure 5   **Figure 6**

3. Mark and stitch three ⅝" buttonholes centered on the button flap 3" apart referring to Figure 6.

4. Slip one 11" x 18" batting piece inside the A-D unit, smoothing batting edge against button flap seam. Baste layers and quilt close to seams using a walking foot; trim batting. Trim length to 16½" to make upper pillow back.

5. Stitch five A strips right sides together lengthwise to one 18" side of E to make A-E unit; press seams toward E.

6. Fold A-E unit in half wrong sides together along A/E seam and press. Smooth remaining 11" x 18" batting piece inside the folded A-E unit. Baste and quilt close to seams using a walking foot; trim batting. Trim length to 16½" to make lower pillow back.

Completing the Pillow

1. With strips vertical on pillow front, position upper pillow back, with strips horizontal, right sides together at the top of pillow front, raw edges even as shown in Figure 7.

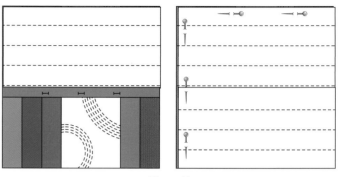

Figure 7

2. Position the lower pillow back, overlapping upper pillow back, on bottom of pillow front with raw edges even and right sides together, again referring Figure 7; pin in place.

3. Stitch around outer edge of pillow. Stitch again ⅛" from original stitching to reinforce seam. Trim corners and finish seam allowance with zigzag, overedge stitch or serger

4. Turn the pillow right side out through the over-lapped back pieces. Use buttonholes as placement guides and hand-stitch three buttons in place. Insert pillow form and close buttons to finish. ■

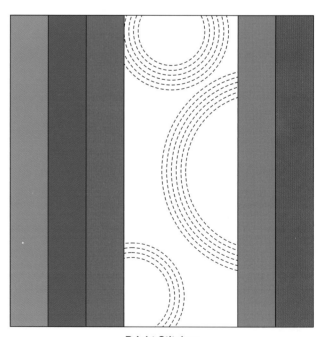

Bright Stitches
Placement Diagram 16" x 16"

Instant Classic

Design by Tricia Lynn Maloney

A traditional block pattern like this Dresden Plate, plus a great fabric line, equals an instant classic.

Project Specifications
Skill Level: Confident Beginner
Pillow Size: 16" x 16"

Project Note
Use 6–12 coordinating print scraps from your stash for the appliqué pieces instead of cutting from fat eighths or yardage. All other pieces can be cut from fat quarters or yardage.

Materials
Note: Materials and instructions listed are for one pillow.

- 1 fat eighth (or ¼ yard) each of 6 coordinating prints
- 1 fat quarter (or ½ yard) floral
- 1 fat quarter (or ⅜ yard) coordinating tonal
- ⅝ yard muslin
- Batting 18" x 18"
- Neutral-color all-purpose thread
- Quilting thread
- Template material
- 16"-square pillow form
- ½" or larger vintage button
- Fabric basting spray (optional)
- Basic sewing tools and supplies

Cutting
1. Prepare E template with pattern provided and template material. Trace two E shapes onto wrong side of each coordinating print fat eighth. Cut out on traced lines to cut a total of 12.

2. From floral fat quarter, cut two 11" x 16½" D rectangles for pillow back.

3. From coordinating tonal fat quarter, cut four 6½" A squares and two each 2½" x 12½" B borders and 2½" x 16½" C borders.

4. Cut one 18" muslin backing square.

Completing the Pillow
1. Fold E in half right sides together and sew across top edge as shown in Figure 1. Turn E right side out, gently pushing out point, and press, again referring to Figure 1. Repeat with all E pieces.

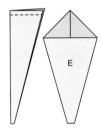

Figure 1

2. Arrange and sew three E pieces together to make an E unit as shown in Figure 2. Press seams in one direction. Repeat to make four E units.

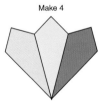

Figure 2   **Figure 3**

3. Position and pin an E unit on the right side of an A square as shown in Figure 3, matching raw edges. Repeat to make four A-E units.

4. Arrange and stitch A-E units together matching E points at seams referring to Figure 4. Press seams open to lessen bulk at center.

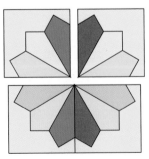

Figure 4

5. Topstitch E unit points in place using a machine straight stitch or a machine- or hand-embroidery decorative stitch to complete pillow top center.

6. Stitch B borders to opposite sides and C borders to top and bottom of pillow top center referring to Placement Diagram; press seams toward borders.

7. Layer backing square, wrong side up, batting and pillow top, right side up and baste with fabric basting spray, thread or pins. Quilt as desired. Trim backing and batting even with pillow top.

8. Fold and press ¼" to wrong side of 16½" edge of D twice to make a double-turned ¼" hem as shown in Figure 5 and edgestitch along first fold. Repeat with second D piece.

Figure 5

9. Position and pin D pieces right sides together with quilted pillow top, matching raw edges and overlapping hemmed edges as shown in Figure 6.

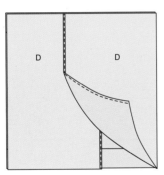

Figure 6

10. Stitch around all edges. Trim corners and finish raw edges with zigzag, overedge stitch or serger.

11. Turn pillow right side out, pushing out corners, and press flat. Edgestitch around pillow. Insert 16"-square pillow form to complete. ■

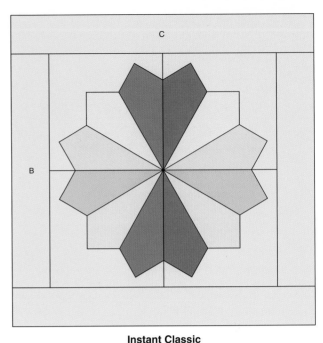

Instant Classic
Placement Diagram 16" x 16"

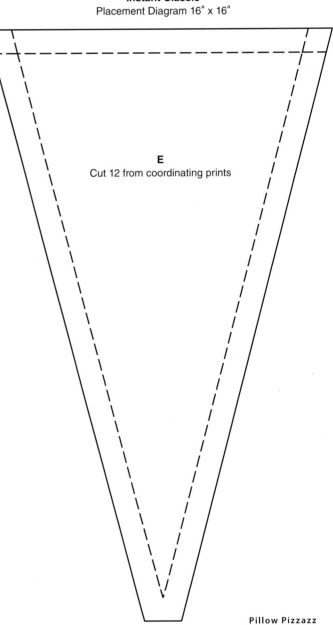

E
Cut 12 from coordinating prints

Pillow Pizzazz

Modern Matches

Design by Carolyn S. Vagts for The Village Pattern Company

These modern pillows can be made out of your scrap basket, or pick a color theme to complete a room decor.

Project Specifications
Skill Level: Confident Beginner
Pillow Size: 20" x 20"

Materials
Note: Materials and instructions listed are for one pillow.

- Assorted batik fat quarters:
    1 each dark, medium and light same color
    1 each light and dark contrasting color
- ¼ yard white solid
- ¾ yard white muslin
- 1⅜ yards coordinating batik
- Batting 22" x 22"
- Thread
- 20"-square pillow form
- Basic sewing tools and supplies

Cutting

1. Cut two 1½" x 22" same-color dark batik fat quarter strips; subcut strips into one each 1½" x 18½" B and O strips.

2. From same-color medium batik fat quarter, cut one strip each 1½" x 22", 2" x 22" and 2½" x 22". Subcut strips into one each 1½" x 16½" F, 2" x 15½" M and 2½" x 15½" H strips.

3. From same-color light batik fat quarter, cut one strip each 1½" x 22" and 2" x 22" light strips. Subcut strips into one each 1½" x 14½" D and 2" x 16½" K strips.

4. From contrasting-color light batik fat quarter, cut one strip 1½" x 22" and two strips 2" x 22". Subcut strips into one each 1½" x 18½" L, 2" x 15½" E and 2" x 18½" I strips.

5. From contrasting-color dark batik fat quarter, cut two strips each 1½" x 22" and 2" x 22". Subcut strips into one each 1½" x15½" J, 1½" x 16½" N, 2" x 16½" C and 2" x 17½" G.

6. Cut two 1½" by fabric width white solid strips; subcut strips into two 1½" x 20½" A and P strips, and

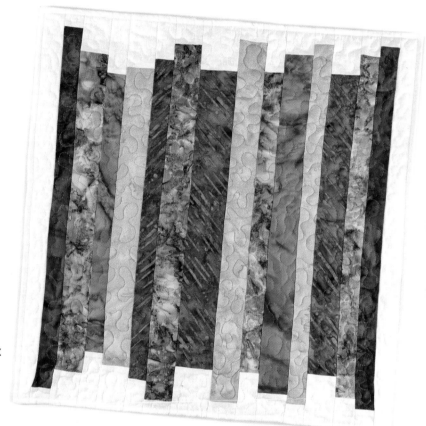

two each 1½" B, L and O squares; 1½" x 2½" F and N rectangles; 1½" x 3" J rectangles; and1½" x 3½" D rectangles; and 1½" x 2" I rectangles.

7. Cut one 2½" by fabric width white solid strips; subcut strip into two each 2" x 2½" C and K, and two 2½" x 3" H rectangles.

8. Trim remainder of strip cut in step 7 to 2" wide and subcut strip into two each 2" x 3" E and M rectangles and two 2" G squares.

9. Cut two 20½" by fabric width coordinating batik rectangles; subcut strips into two 20½" x 27" Q rectangles.

10. Cut one 22" white muslin backing square.

Completing the Pillow

1. Stitch corresponding white solid pieces to opposite ends of assorted batik fat quarter strips to make 20½" long B–O pieced strips. For example, stitch 1½" white B squares to opposite ends of 1½" x 18½" dark batik B strip as shown in Figure 1.

Figure 1

2. Arrange pieced B–O strips referring to Placement Diagram. Add A strip to top and P strip to bottom of arrangement.

3. Stitch A–P strips together on 20½" sides in alphabetical order, again referring to the Placement Diagram. Press seams in one direction.

4. Layer muslin backing square, batting and pillow top with right side up. Baste with basting spray, thread or pins, and quilt as desired. Trim backing and batting even with pillow top.

5. Fold Q rectangles in half wrong sides together to make two 20½" x 14" Q pillow backs and press.

6. Position and pin Q pillow backs right sides together with quilted pillow top, matching raw edges and overlapping pressed edges as shown in Figure 2.

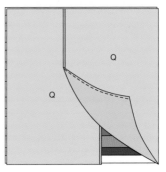

Figure 2

7. Stitch around all edges. Trim corners and finish raw edges with zigzag, overedge stitch or serger.

8. Turn pillow right side out, pushing out corners, and press edges flat. Topstitch ¼" from outer edge and insert pillow form to complete. ■

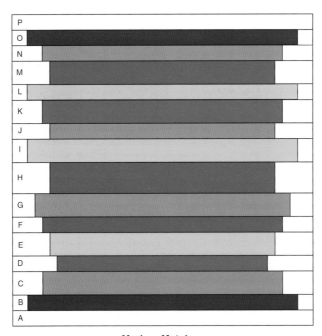

Modern Matches
Placement Diagram 20" x 20"

Spring

Design by Lynn Weglarz

Got fun fabrics? Make a set of blooming accent pillows.

Project Specifications
Skill Level: Confident Beginner
Pillow Size: 18" x 18"

Project Notes
The project "Spring" is a creative accent pillow, and the instructions are intended as a springboard for creating a bouquet of simple flowers. By varying colors and sizes of flower circles, using curved or straight stems cut to different lengths and by adding leaves to fill out the bouquet, you can create your own special arrangements. Refer to photos, figure drawings and the Placement Diagram for ideas.

This is also a great project to practice fusible appliqué and adding decorative embellishments. Follow the manufacturer's instructions with the fusible web you choose to use for fusible appliqué. Use different decorative hand-embroidery stitches, referring to the basic stitch diagrams included here, and add beads and buttons to give your flowers depth.

Materials
- Variety bright scraps or fat quarters for appliqué flowers, stems and leaves
- ⅔ yard white tonal
- ⅔ yard white muslin
- Lightweight batting 20" x 20"
- 18"-square pillow form
- ½ yard paper-backed fusible web
- 1 (20–22") white invisible or regular zipper
- Variety thread
- White quilting thread
- Black cotton embroidery floss
- Variety ¾" or larger decorative buttons
- Variety seed beads
- Chenille/embroidery hand needles
- Beading needles
- Template material
- Fabric basting spray (optional)
- Basic sewing tools and supplies

Cutting
1. Prepare templates from patterns given for flower circles and leaves. Trace a variety of flower circles and leaves on the paper side of fusible web. Draw several ⅜"–¼" x 17" curved or straight stems on paper side of fusible web. Cut out shapes approximately ⅛" away from traced lines.

2. Following the manufacturer's instructions, fuse shapes to wrong side of scraps for flower circles, leaves and stems. Cut out shapes on traced lines.

3. Cut one 20" by fabric width strip white tonal; subcut strip into one 20" pillow front A square and two 10¼" x 19" pillow back B rectangles.

4. Cut one 20" backing square from white muslin.

Completing the Pillow
1. Layer batting between wrong side of pillow front A and muslin backing square. Spray- or thread-baste layers together and free-motion–quilt as desired.

2. Trim quilted pillow front to 19" square.

3. Layer circles to make flowers and arrange with leaves and stems on the A side of quilted pillow front as desired and referring to Placement Diagram. Fuse in place following manufacturer's instructions.

4. Machine-stitch stems in place using a zigzag or straight stitch and free-motion–quilt some of the inner circles in place as shown in Figure 1.

Figure 1

5. Add hand-embroidery stitches to flowers and leaves referring to Basic Embroidery Stitch diagrams, on page 32, and photos. Add other embellishments such as buttons or beads as desired.

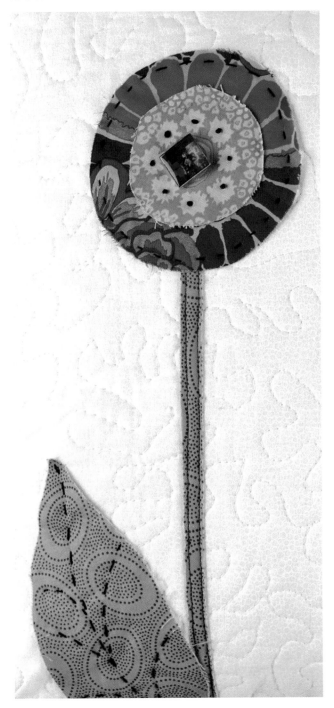

6. Center and sew zipper between two B rectangles following manufacturer's instructions for centered zipper application to make pillow back.

7. Trim completed pillow back to 19" square with zipper positioned in center as shown in Figure 2.

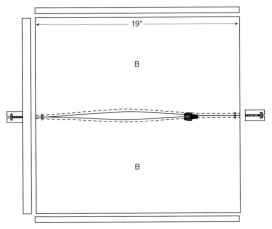

Figure 2

8. Move zipper pull to center of pillow back and stitch across zipper ends ¼" from back edges to secure, again referring to Figure 2.

9. Stitch pillow front to back, right sides together, with a ½" seam allowance, making sure to leave the zipper partially open. Trim corners and finish raw edges with zigzag, overedge stitches or serger.

10. Turn pillow right side out, press seams and insert pillow form. ■

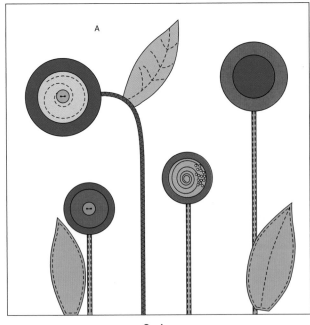

Spring
Placement Diagram 18" x 18"

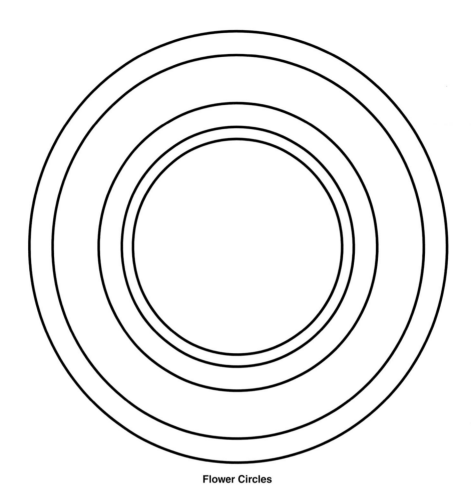

Flower Circles

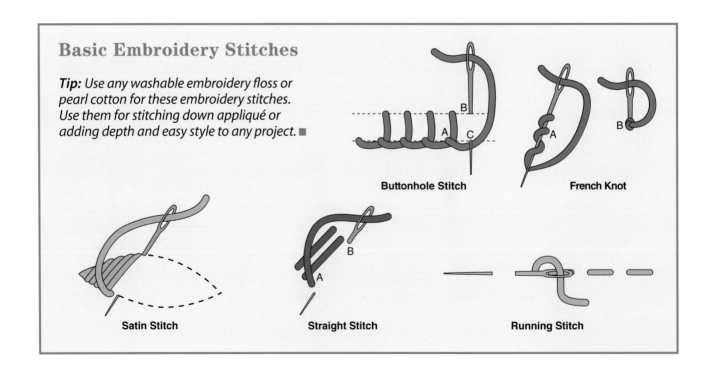

Basic Embroidery Stitches

Tip: Use any washable embroidery floss or pearl cotton for these embroidery stitches. Use them for stitching down appliqué or adding depth and easy style to any project. ■

Buttonhole Stitch

French Knot

Satin Stitch

Straight Stitch

Running Stitch

Pillow Pizzazz

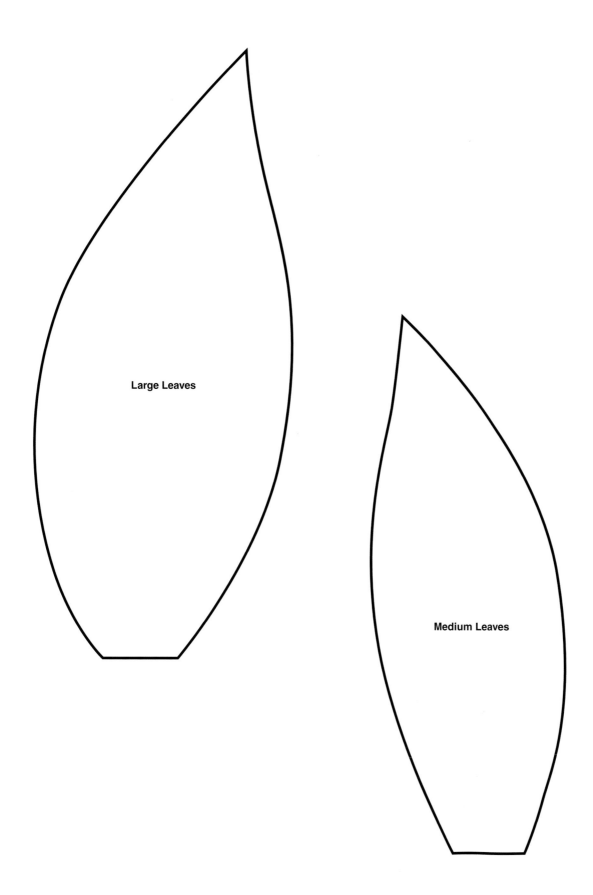

Large Leaves

Medium Leaves

Annie's, Berne, Indiana 46711   Clotilde.com

Squared Up

Design by Julie Weaver

Precut strips and an accent fabric make this tailored
pillow a conversation piece on your sofa.

Project Specifications

Skill Level: Confident Beginner
Pillow Size: 18" x 18"

Materials

*Note: Materials and instructions listed are for
one pillow.*

- 15 precut 2½" batik strips
- 1 yard 45"-wide lightweight batting
- 1⅛ yards coordinating fabric
- 18"-square pillow form
- 2½" covered button
- Long straight upholstery needle
- Upholstery thread
- Thread
- Fabric basting spray (optional)
- Basic sewing tools and supplies

Cutting

1. Cut each batik strip in half to make 30 strips at
least 20½" long.

2. Cut one 18½" by fabric width strip coordinating
fabric; subcut strip into cut one 18½" A lining square
and two 10½" x 18½" B lining rectangles.

3. Cut one 10" by fabric width strip of coordinating
fabric; subcut strip into two 10" C lining squares.

4. Cut three 2½" by fabric width strips coordinating
fabric for binding.

5. Cut one 22" x 42" rectangle and two 10½" x 18½"
rectangles from lightweight batting.

Completing the Pillow Back

1. Select and sew nine batik strips right sides
together lengthwise. Trim strip set to 18½" square
for pillow center back.

2. Select and sew five strips right sides together
lengthwise to make one pillow point strip set. Trim
strip set to 10½" x 18½" for pillow point. Repeat to
make two pillow points.

3. Mark center of both 18½" edges on wrong side of
pillow point section and ¼" up from bottom 18½"
edge. Draw a line connecting center marks and ¼"
marks as shown in Figure 1.

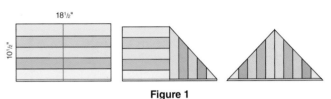

Figure 1

4. Fold and press top right corner to the bottom
center wrong sides together along ¼" marked line
above bottom edge, again referring to Figure 1.
Repeat with top left corner.

5. Unfold corners and rotary-trim along pressed line
as shown in Figure 2.

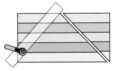

Figure 2

6. Repeat steps 3–5 to make a second pillow point.

7. Using a trimmed pillow point as a pattern, cut
two pillow point linings from the C lining pieces.
Set aside for pillow front.

8. Sew a pillow point to opposite sides of the center
back square cut in step 1, right sides together as
shown in Figure 3. Press seams toward center.

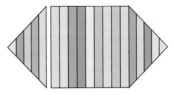

Figure 3

9. Layer and spray-baste assembled pillow back, wrong side up, with 22" x 42" batting rectangle. Trim batting to pillow back shape. Position the A lining square on top of batting, wrong side down and centered over 18½" center back square as shown in Figure 4.

Figure 4

10. Stitching with pillow center back on top, quilt in-the-ditch along each seam and ½" on either side of the seams referring to Figure 5. *Note: Do not quilt in-the-ditch on the seam between the center back square and points as indicated by the red arrow.*

Figure 5

Completing the Pillow Front

1. Select and sew five strips right sides together lengthwise to make one 10½" pillow front strip set. Trim strip set to 10½" x 18½" for pillow front. Repeat to make two pillow fronts.

2. Sew B lining rectangles and pillow fronts, right sides together, along one 18½" side as shown in Figure 6. Press pillow fronts to right side.

Figure 6

3. Insert a 10½" x 18½" batting piece between pillow front and lining on both pillow fronts. Quilt each piece referring to step 10 and Figure 5 of Completing the Pillow Back.

4. Overlap stitched edges of pillow fronts approximately 1" and pin in place as shown in Figure 7.

Figure 7

5. Sew a C pillow point lining, right sides together, on opposite overlapped edges as shown in Figure 8. Press seams toward C.

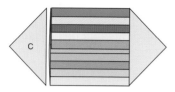

Figure 8

8. Position pillow back on pillow front, wrong sides together. Pin pillow points together, leaving pillow front and back centers loose.

9. With pillow back on top, quilt pillow points only referring to step 10 and Figure 5 of Completing the Pillow Back, beginning with the seam between the center and points as shown in Figure 9.

Figure 9

Completing the Pillow

1. Join binding strips on short ends with diagonal seams to make one long strip; trim seams to ¼" and press seams open.

2. Fold and press the binding strip in half wrong sides together along length.

3. Sew binding to pillow back edges, matching raw edges, mitering corners and overlapping ends.

4. Fold binding to pillow front and stitch in place to finish.

5. Insert pillow form through pillow center front and hand-stitch opening closed.

6. Fold pillow points toward center of pillow front and adjust so strips form squares with center front strips as shown in Figure 10. Hand-stitch points together to hold in place.

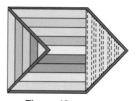

Figure 10

7. Cover 2½" button with coordinating fabric remnant.

8. Using upholstery needle and upholstery thread, insert needle from back to front, catching shank on button and knotting on pillow back to finish. ∎

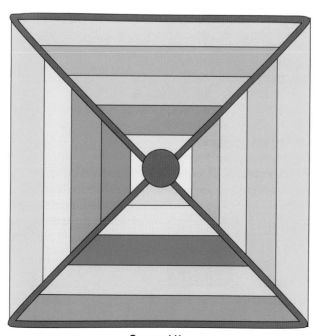

Squared Up
Placement Diagram 18" x 18"

Rainbow Pillows

Designs by Connie Rand

Create your own rainbow with strips and a bit of appliqué. It looks harder than it actually is.

Project Specifications
Skill Level: Confident Beginner
Pillow Size: 16" x 16"

Materials
Note: *Materials and instructions listed are for one pillow.*

- 1 fat quarter each in 5 different shades (lightest, light, medium, dark, darkest) of blue, green, yellow-orange and red tonals or prints
- ⅝ yard coordinating tonal or print
- Batting 16½" x 16½"
- 16"-square pillow form
- Thread
- Basic sewing tools and supplies

Cutting
1. Cut two 1½" x 8½" strips each lightest and darkest red, blue, yellow-orange and green.

2. Cut three 1½" x 8½" strips each light, medium and dark red, blue, yellow-orange and green.

3. Cut one 16½" square for quilting backing and two 8¾" x 16½" rectangles for pillow back from coordinating tonal or print.

Completing Pillow
1. Join eight 1½" x 8½" strips as shown in Figure 1 using one each darkest and lightest strip, and two each of the light, medium and dark shades of same color. Make one set of strips for each color.

Figure 1

2. Join strip sets referring to Figure 2 for color placement and orientation. Set aside for pillow front background.

Figure 2

3. Join five 1½" x 8½" strips of one color, lightest to darkest shades, as shown in Figure 3. Make one set of strips for each color.

Figure 3

4. Trim each color set to make a 5½" square, again referring to Figure 3.

5. Join strip set squares referring to Figure 4 for color placement and orientation to make the center unit.

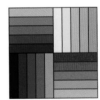

Figure 4

6. Prepare a circle pattern using template provided. Center and cut a circle from the center unit referring to Figure 5 and staystitch ⅛" from the edge of the circle.

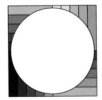

Figure 5

7. Turn and press circle edge ¼" to wrong side. Pin the circle to the pillow front center, aligning the seams and referring to the Placement Diagram for placement, and appliqué in place by hand or machine.

8. Layer quilting backing square wrong side up, batting, and pillow front right side up. Quilt as desired by hand or machine.

9. Turn ¼" to wrong side on one 16½" edge of each pillow back rectangle. Repeat and stitch to make a double-turned ¼" hem on both pillow back rectangles.

10. Position and pin pillow back rectangles right sides together with quilted pillow top, matching raw edges and overlapping hemmed edges as shown in Figure 6.

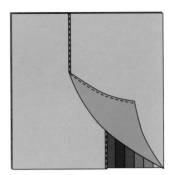

Figure 6

11. Stitch around all outside edges using a ¼" seam allowance. Trim corners and finish seam allowance with zigzag or overedge stitch.

12. Turn right side out and insert 16"-square pillow form to complete pillow. ■

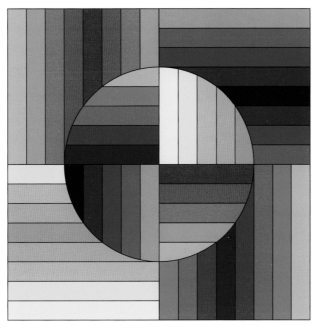

Rainbow Pillows
Placement Diagram
16" x 16"

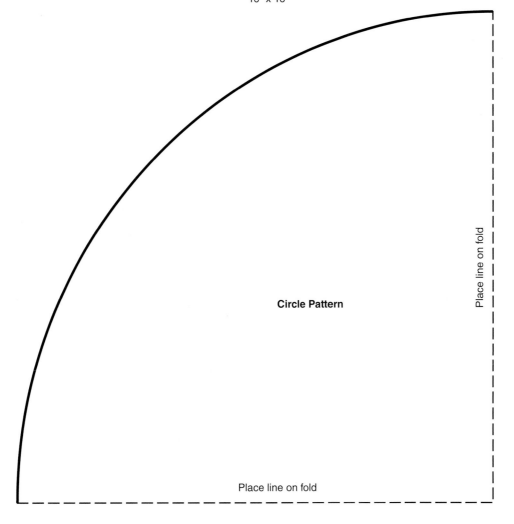

Place line on fold

Circle Pattern

Place line on fold

Annie's, Berne, Indiana 46711   Clotilde.com

Cabins

Design by Tricia Lynn Maloney

Log Cabin blocks never go out of style and can accent any decor with savvy fabric choices.

Project Specifications
Skill Level: Beginner
Finished Size: 20" x 20"

Materials
Note: Materials and instructions listed are for one pillow.

- ⅛ yard or fat quarter each:
  red solid
  B, C, D coordinating lights
  E, F, G coordinating darks
- ¾ yard muslin
- ⅞ yard coordinating print
- Batting 22" x 22"
- 20"-square pillow form
- Thread
- Fabric basting spray (optional)
- Basic sewing tools and supplies

Cutting
1. Cut one 2½" by fabric width strip red solid; subcut strip into four 2½" A squares.

2. Cut one 1½" by fabric width strip from each B and C coordinating light fabrics. Cut two 1½" by fabric width strips from the D coordinating light fabric. Subcut strips into four each: B1 (1½" x 2½"), B2 (1½" x 3½"), C5 (1½" x 4½"), C6 (1½" x 5½"), D9 (1½" x 6½") and D10 (1½" x 7½") rectangles.

3. Cut one 1½" by fabric width strip from the E coordinating dark fabric. Cut two 1½" by fabric width strips from each F and G coordinating dark fabrics. Subcut strips into four each: E3 (1½" x 3½"), E4 (1½" x 4½"), F7 (1½" x 5½"), F8 (1½" x 6½"), G11 (1½" x 7½") and G12 (1½" x 8½") rectangles.

4. Cut two 2½" by fabric width strips coordinating print; subcut strips into two 2½" x 16½" H borders and two 2½" x 20½" I borders.

5. Cut one 21" by fabric width strip coordinating print; subcut strip into two 13" x 21" J rectangles.

6. Cut one 22" muslin backing square.

Completing the Pillow
1. Select one each of A and B1–G12 strips. Stitch strips in a counterclockwise direction around A in the order shown in Figure 1 beginning with B1 at top of A to make one Log Cabin block. Press seams away from A center square. Repeat to make four blocks.

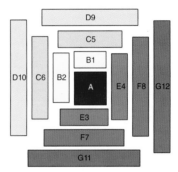

Figure 1

2. Stitch blocks together matching dark sides of Log Cabin design as shown in Figure 2.

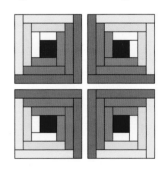

Figure 2

3. Stitch H borders to top and bottom, and I borders to sides of the pieced center referring to Placement Diagram; press seams toward borders.

4. Layer muslin backing square, batting and pillow top with right side up. Baste with basting spray, thread or pins, and quilt as desired. Trim backing and batting even with pillow top.

5. Fold and press ¼" to the wrong side of 21" edge of J twice to make a double-turned ¼" hem as shown in Figure 3; edgestitch along first fold. Repeat with second J piece.

Figure 3

6. Position and pin J pieces right sides together with quilted pillow top, matching raw edges and overlapping hemmed edges as shown in Figure 4.

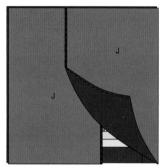

Figure 4

7. Stitch around all edges. Trim corners and finish raw edges with zigzag, overedge stitch or serger.

8. Turn pillow right side out and insert 20"-square pillow form. ■

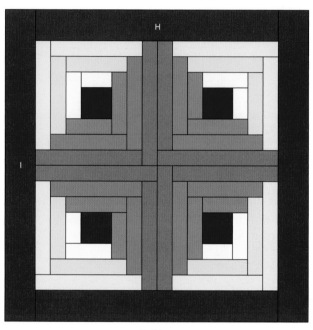

Cabins
Placement Diagram 20" x 20"

'Tis the Season

Design by Gina Gempesaw

Add a touch of the holidays to a chair or a sofa. Deck the halls and be merry.

Project Specifications
Skill Level: Confident Beginner
Pillow Size: 14" x 14"

Materials
Note: Materials and instructions listed are for one pillow.

- ⅛ yard red tonal
- ¼ yard gold tonal
- ⅜ yard green tonal
- 1⅛ yards coordinating print
- Batting 17" x 17"
- 14"-square pillow form
- Thread
- Fabric basting spray (optional)
- Basic sewing tools and supplies

Cutting
1. Cut one 3¼" by fabric width strip red tonal; subcut four 3¼" A squares.

2. Cut one 3½" by fabric width strip gold tonal; subcut strip into four 3½" x 6½" F rectangles. Trim remainder of strip to 3¼" and subcut one 3¼" E square.

3. Cut one 3¼" by fabric width strip green tonal; subcut strip into four 3¼" B squares and four 3¼" x 6" C rectangles.

4. Cut two 3" by fabric width strips green tonal; subcut strips into eight 3" x 5½" rectangles. Cut four rectangles diagonally from top left corner to bottom right corner for eight D1 triangles as shown in Figure 1. Cut remaining four rectangles diagonally from top right corner to bottom left corner for eight D2 triangles, again referring to Figure 1.

Figure 1

5. Cut one 18" by fabric width strip coordinating print; subcut strip into two 14½" x 18" G rectangles.

6. Cut one 17" backing square from coordinating print.

Completing the Pillow
1. Select one each A, B and C; with right sides together sew A and B together to make an A-B unit; press seam. Sew C to the A-B unit as shown in Figure 2 to complete a corner unit. Repeat to make four corner units.

Figure 2

2. Make four copies of the D-F Unit Paper-Piecing Pattern provided.

3. Referring to Paper Piecing, on page 48, use D1, D2 and F pieces to paper-piece four D-F units as shown in Figure 3. Trim units to 3¼" x 6".

Figure 3

4. Referring to Figure 4 for positioning throughout, stitch E between two D-F units to make a center row. Stitch a D-F unit between two corner units to make a top row; repeat to make a bottom row. Sew rows together to make pillow top, again referring to Figure 4.

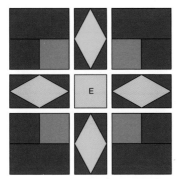

Figure 4

5. Layer 17" backing square, wrong side up; add batting and pillow top, right side up and baste layers together using fabric basting spray, thread or pins.

6. Quilt as desired. Trim backing and batting even with pillow top.

7. Fold and press both G pieces in half, wrong sides together, to make two G rectangles 14½" x 9".

8. Position and pin G rectangles right sides together with quilted pillow top matching raw edges and overlapping pressed edges as shown in Figure 5. Pin and stitch around raw edges.

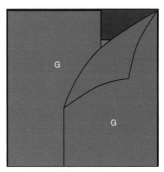

Figure 5

9. Trim corners and finish seams with zigzag, over-edge stitches or serger. Turn pillow right side out.

10. Insert 14"-square pillow form. ∎

'Tis the Season
Placement Diagram 14" x 14"

Annie's, Berne, Indiana 46711 Clotilde.com

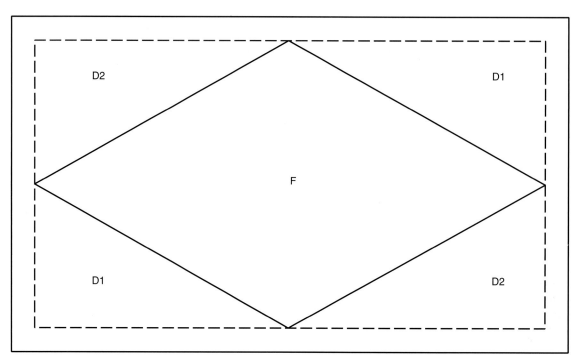

D-F Unit Paper-Piecing Pattern
Make 4 copies

Paper Piecing

One of the oldest quilting techniques, paper piecing allows a quilter to make blocks with odd-shaped and/or small pieces. The paper is carefully removed when the block is completed. The following instructions are for one type of paper-piecing technique; refer to a comprehensive quilting guide for other types of paper piecing.

1. Make same-size photocopies of the paper-piecing pattern given as directed on the pattern. There are several choices in regular papers as well as water-soluble papers that can be used, which are available at your local office-supply store, quilt shop or online.

2. Cut out the patterns, leaving a margin around the outside bold lines as shown in Figure 1. Pattern color choices can be written in each numbered space on the

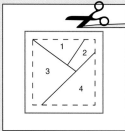

Figure 1

marked side of each. All patterns are reversed on the paper copies.

3. With the printed side of the pattern facing you, fold along each line of the pattern as shown in Figure 2, creasing the stitching lines. This will help in trimming the fabric seam allowances and in removing the paper when you are finished stitching.

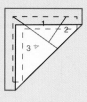 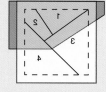

Figure 2   **Figure 3**

4. Turn the paper pattern over with the unmarked side facing you and position fabric indicated on pattern right side up over the space marked 1. Hold the paper up to a window or over a light box to make sure that the fabric overlaps all sides of space 1 at least ¼", as shown in Figure 3, from the printed side of the pattern. Pin or use a light touch of glue stick to hold fabric in place.

5. Turn the paper over with the right side of the paper facing you, and fold the paper along the lines between sections 1 and 2. Trim fabric to about ¼" from the folded edge as shown in Figure 4.

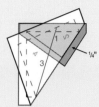

Figure 4

6. Place the second fabric indicated right sides together with the first piece. Fabric edges should be even along line between spaces 1 and 2 as shown in Figure 5. Fold fabric over and check to see if second fabric piece will cover space 2.

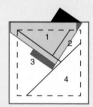

Figure 5

7. With the right side of the paper facing you, hold fabric pieces together and stitch along the line between spaces 1 and 2 as shown in Figure 6 using a very small stitch length (18 to 20 stitches per inch). *Note: Using a smaller stitch length will make removing paper easier because it creates a tear line at the seam.* Always begin and end seam by sewing two to three stitches beyond the line. You do not need to backstitch. When the beginning of the seam is at the edge of the pattern, start sewing at the solid outside line of the pattern.

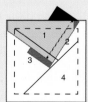

Figure 6

8. Turn the pattern over, flip the second fabric back and finger-press as shown in Figure 7.

Figure 7

9. Continue trimming and sewing pieces in numerical order until the pattern is completely covered. Make sure pieces along the outer edge extend past the solid line to allow for a ¼" seam allowance as shown in Figure 8.

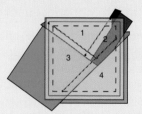

Figure 8

10. When the whole block is sewn, press the block and trim all excess fabric from the block along the outside-edge solid line of paper pattern as shown in Figure 9.

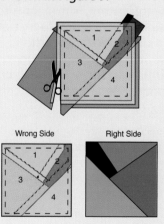

Wrong Side   Right Side

Figure 9

11. Carefully remove backing paper from completed block and press seams. ∎

Simple Whole-Cloth Pillows

By Carolyn S. Vagts

Turn a single piece of solid fabric into a beautiful accent pillow and practice your machine quilting at the same time.

Designer Notes

I have always loved the look of traditional whole-cloth quilts and have admired the dedication that goes into them. Even so, I've never found the time or the patience to attempt one—until now.

Machine-quilting and making a 16" pillow instead of a full-size quilt reduces the time element of a whole-cloth project considerably. Like many quilters, I love to take a traditional technique and tweak it. So, using one of today's popular, crisp solid colors instead of traditional white or natural muslin tweaks the whole-cloth technique just enough to suit my creative side.

Now I can play with an intriguing technique on a level that won't tax my patience, dedication or wallet. To play along, gather the following materials and follow the cutting instructions for one 16" pillow. Double the materials to try both of the quilting designs included in this article.

Project Specifications

Skill Level: Confident Beginner
Pillow Size: 16" x 16"

Materials

Note: Materials and instructions listed are for one pillow.

- 1 yard solid color
- Batting 18" x 18"
- 16"-square pillow form
- Thread
- Fabric basting spray
- Water-soluble marking tool
- 1"–2"-wide blue painter's tape
- Graph paper and pencil
- Walking or even-feed sewing machine foot
- Basic sewing tools and supplies

Cutting

1. Cut two 18" x fabric width strips solid color; subcut one strip into one 17" square for pillow top and one 17" x 18" rectangle.

2. Subcut remaining strip into one 18" backing square and one 17" x 18" rectangle.

Quilting Techniques

If you are a beginning quilter or new to machine quilting, try the masking-tape method first. The tape is placed on the project and used as a stitching guide. If you are a bit more experienced then try the free-motion quilting method. Pillows are the perfect size to experiment on. Both techniques are fun and easy to handle, and both offer a great finished look.

Masking-Tape Method

Start planning your quilting design by sketching out ideas on graph paper. Consider the finished size of the pillow—16" square for this project—and the width of the tape you will use. Your pattern should fit within the finished size and the distance between lines is determined by the width of tape used.

> *Tip*
> *Read the instructions on your batting and space your quilting lines no farther apart than suggested by the manufacturer.*

I have chosen a simple grid using 1½"-wide tape on a 16" square as shown in Figure 1. **Note:** *Don't forget that you will actually be working with a 17" square for the pillow top. This includes the seam allowances.*

Once you have decided on your quilting pattern, use a water-soluble marking tool to transfer the measurements of your pattern to the edges of the 17" solid-color square as shown in Figure 2.

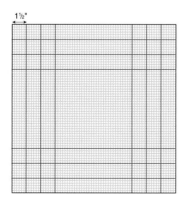

Figure 1

Figure 2

Annie's, Berne, Indiana 46711   Clotilde.com

Completing the Pillow Top

1. With the 18" backing square wrong side up, place the batting on top; center the marked 17" pillow top square, right side up, on top of the batting. Baste layers together using fabric basting spray referring to the manufacturer's instructions to make a quilt sandwich.

2. Make a stitching guide by aligning a piece of tape, longer than the pillow, across the pillow connecting the edge marks for an interior line of the quilting design as shown in Figure 3. Use a walking or even-feed foot to slowly stitch along both sides of the tape. ***Note:*** *I also have used an open-toe embroidery foot because it allows me to see the tape edge clearly. The walking foot works well because it moves all fabric layers through the machine evenly which virtually eliminates tucks.*

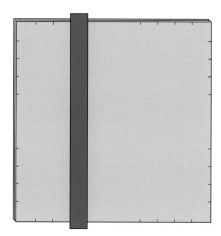

Figure 3

3. Once you have stitched along the tape edges, carefully remove it and realign it, connecting the next edge marks as shown in Figure 4. Continue in this manner until you have stitched all quilting design lines from the center out.

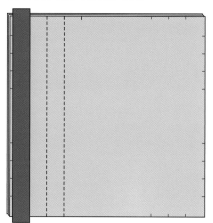

Figure 4

4. Trim batting and backing even with pillow top, squaring if necessary to 17".

5. Finish pillow according to Completing the Pillow on page 54.

Free-Motion Design Method

Pillow tops provide a manageable size to try out new free-motion designs. If you are thinking of quilting a quilt with a certain motif, why not try it first on a pillow? If it works out, you have a matching pillow to go with your quilt, or a great gift.

Tip

This also is a great way to try out stencils. Use a water-soluble marker and lay out your pattern with the stencil and then machine-quilt. It's a great way to increase your control and speed.

Draw the design on plain paper. Play with the design until you are happy and like the way it flows from one motif to the next in a continuous pattern like the motif I drew as shown in Figure 5.

Figure 5

Establish stop points in the design to rest and change directions. If you have stop points, you will be able to go from one motif to the next smoothly and you will know when you can take a break to rethink where to go next. The red X's mark the spots in Figure 5 where I have chosen to rest and change directions in my design. Practice your design by tracing it several times, stopping and changing directions at your chosen stop points.

After practicing on paper, prepare a quilt sandwich from scraps. Starting somewhere in the middle of the scrap quilt sandwich, pull your bobbin thread up to the top. Pull both your bobbin and top thread tails behind the machine foot out of the way. Start stitching your motif design resting at your stop point to trim off the thread tails; continue quilting. Practice until you are comfortable with the movement and look of your design (Figure 6).

Figure 6

Completing the Pillow Top

1. With the 18" backing square, wrong side up, place the batting on top; center the marked 17" pillow top square, right side up, on top of the batting. Baste layers together using fabric basting spray referring to the manufacturer's instructions to make a quilt sandwich.

2. Beginning at the pillow top center, start free-motion quilting referring to the practicing steps above and quilt the entire pillow top.

3. Trim batting and backing even with pillow top, squaring if necessary to 17".

Completing the Pillow

1. Fold and press both 17" x 18" rectangles wrong sides together to make two 17" x 9" pillow backs.

Tip

It's good practice to have a few scrap quilt sandwiches around to check designs and tension. I always start a new free-motion design on a scrap quilt sandwich to see where my resting points will be, and how the thread I have chosen will work with my fabrics and batting. Not all threads are the same. Adjustments to tension are sometimes needed for best results.

2. Position and pin pillow backs right sides together with quilted pillow top, matching raw edges and overlapping pressed edges as shown in Figure 7.

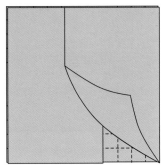

Figure 7

3. Stitch a ½" seam around the edges. Trim corners and finish raw edges with zigzag, overedge stitch or serger.

4. Turn pillow right side out, pushing out corners, and press edges flat.

5. Topstitch ¼" from outer edge and insert pillow form to complete. ∎

Free-Motion Design
Whole-Cloth Pillow
Placement Diagram 16" x 16"

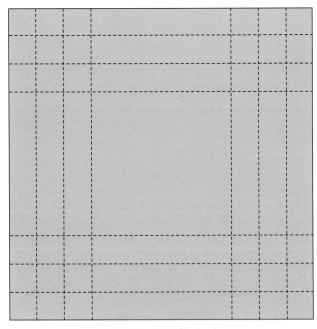

Masking-Tape Method
Whole-Cloth Pillow
Placement Diagram 16" x 16"

Fabric & Supplies

Instant Classic: Francesca collection by Anna Griffin fabrics

Scrappy String Pillows: Warm & Natural cotton batting from The Warm Company

Simple Whole-Cloth Pillows: Moda Bella Solids

Squared Up: Hoffman Fabrics Bali Pops; Hobbs Thermore Batting

'Tis the Season: Stonehenge collection for Northcott Fabrics

Basic Sewing Tools & Supplies

- Sewing machine
- Needles, sizes 9–14 or needle of choice
- Specialty feet (optional)
- Darning foot
- Open-toe embroidery foot
- Walking foot
- Serger (optional)
- Scissors: various sizes and types
- Rotary cutter(s) and mats
- See-through rulers in various sizes
    4½" x 12"
    6½" x 24"
    12½" square

- 45mm rotary cutter
- 18" x 24" or 24" x 36" cutting mat
- Steam/dry iron and ironing board
- Pins
- Glass-head straight pins
- Curved safety pins
- Marking tools (water-soluble or chalk)
- Fabric spray adhesive
- Hand-sewing needles and thimble
- Point turners
- Seam ripper

Annie's™ *Pillow Pizzazz* is published by Annie's, 306 East Parr Road, Berne, IN 46711. Printed in USA. Copyright © 2012 Annie's. All rights reserved. This publication may not be reproduced in part or in whole without written permission from the publisher.

RETAIL STORES: If you would like to carry this pattern book or any other Annie's publications, visit AnniesWSL.com

Every effort has been made to ensure that the instructions in this pattern book are complete and accurate. We cannot, however, take responsibility for human error, typographical mistakes or variations in individual work. Please visit ClotildeCustomerCare.com to check for pattern updates.

ISBN: 978-1-59635-596-5
1 2 3 4 5 6 7 8 9

Photo Index

3

6

10

16

22

19

25

28

34

38

42

45

50